Get Started!
Letters, Numbers, and More!

• Table of Contents •

Counting

- Counting to 20
- Number Order
- Tracing Numbers
- Writing Numbers
- Recognizing Numbers

Counting Parent Tips

Numbers in the Neighborhood

Pick a number of the day and go on a number walk with your child. For example, if you choose the number **4**, look for **4** wheels on a car, **4** streets at an intersection, and so on. You can also have fun playing "I Spy" with your child. Tell your child "I spy the number **5** and it is written in the color *blue*" or "I spy the number **7** and you can find it on a red square", and let him or her look around for what you see. Look for numbers everywhere!

Eat Your Numbers

Play counting games while having a healthy snack. Tell your child you are hungry for **5** grapes, **3** crackers, or **11** blueberries. You can also try making numbers out of different foods. Arrange carrots or celery sticks to make different numbers, or use cooled cooked spaghetti noodles to form curvy numbers. Try tasting crackers, cookies, noodles, cereal, and other items that are shaped like numbers, too.

Get Moving! Number Stretch

Help your child to play safely while learning about numbers. Before exercising, help your child stretch his or her muscles while counting out loud. Encourage your child to touch his or her toes as you count to **12**, or reach for the sky as you count together to **15**. What other fun stretches can you do? Then, exercise and move that body as you count some more. Try **10** sit-ups, **2** push-ups, or **6** jumping jacks. What else can you do to exercise your body? Don't forget to count how many times your heart can beat in one minute!

Count on Clean-up Time

Clean-up time can *be a time* of learning and fun! Encourage your child to clean up toys by gathering them into groups of a certain number. For example, instruct your child to find **3** animal toys or **8** building blocks. Ask your child which group is **bigger** and which group is **smaller**, or which group has **more** and which group has **fewer**. What other comparison words can you use?

Gluey Loopy Numbers

Find some colorful string or yarn, a glue bottle or glue stick, and several pieces of sturdy paper or cardboard. With a pencil, help your child write a large number on one piece of paper, and allow your child to trace over the number with glue. Then, help your child to place the colorful string on top of the glue to form the number. Let it dry and add decorative drawings or items to show how many. You can add feathers, stickers, cotton balls or anything else you choose. For a slightly messy variation, try adding colorful glitter over the glue instead of yarn or string.

 **Tad has 1 snuggly teddy bear.**

 Count and color **1** teddy bear for Tad.

 Trace and write the number **1**.

• 2 •

Leap thinks skateboarding is fun.
Check out his moves!

1-2-3 Count and color **2** skateboards for Leap.

Trace and write the number **2**.

2 2 2

✳Get Moving!

Play **Two** by **Two** by choosing a leader and a follower. The leader will do an action **2** times. Then, the follower must do the action **2** times, too! Try actions like clapping, stomping, twisting, jumping or spinning. Switch leaders and play again! Do it faster!

Lily picked **3** beautiful flowers.
Look out Lily! What does Lily see?

 Color the parts of the puzzle using the code below.

3= ●   **2=** ○   **1=** ●

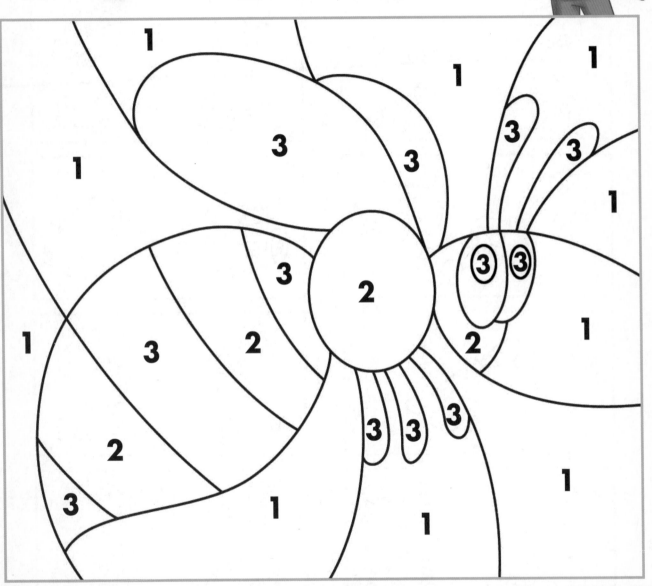

  Trace and write the number **3**.

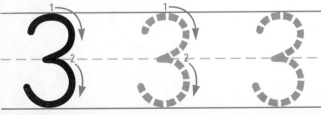

• 4 •

Vroom vroom! Beep beep! Leap and Tad are playing with their cars.

 Count the cars in each group. Then, color each group with **4** cars.

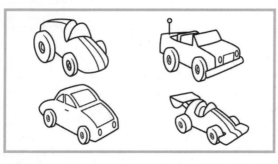

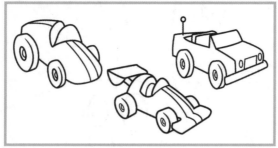

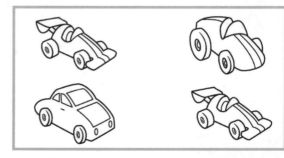

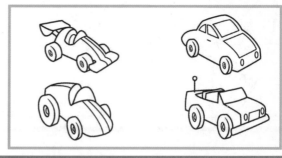

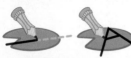 Trace and write the number **4**.

• 5 • Throw it high – throw it low!
Lily and Tad are tossing **5** beanbags.

 Count and color **5** beanbags.

  Trace and write the number **5**.

5 5 5

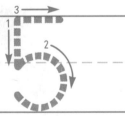

Get Moving!

Give me **5**! Find some space outside for running. Choose a place to start, and choose a place to finish. See if you can make it from the start to the finish before your friend counts to **5**. Take turns counting to **5**, and change the start or end, then run again!

•1-5• How many marbles? Leap and Lily love to play with colorful marbles.

1-2-3 Count the marbles in each group. Draw a line to match the groups with the same number.

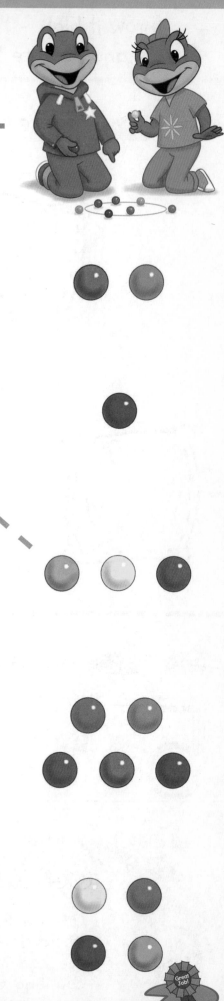

Look at Leap's kite flying in the wind!

  Count and color **6** kites.

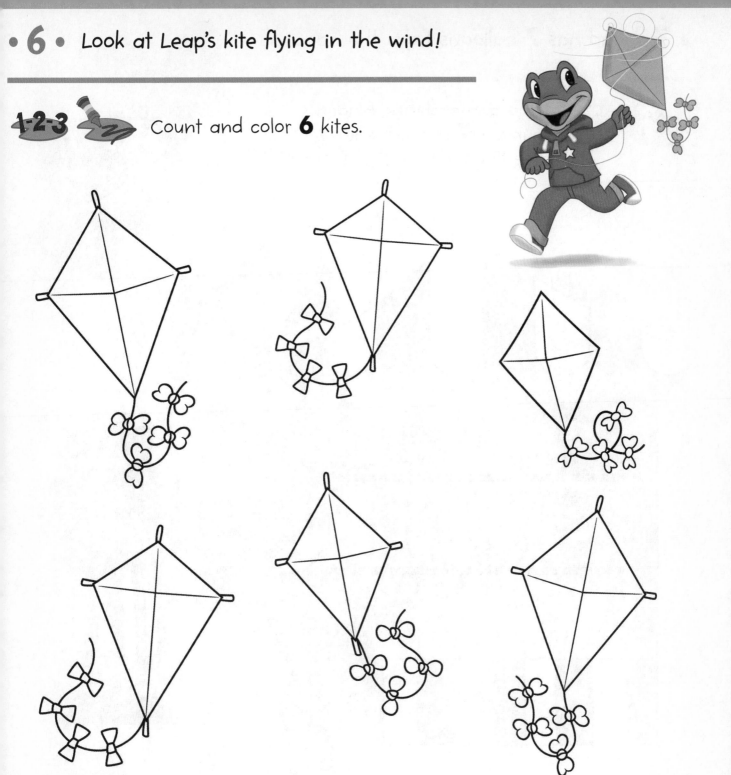

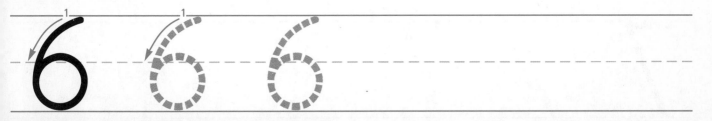 Trace and write the number **6**.

• 7 • Tad has **7** balloons from the carnival.

Find and circle the hidden number **7** in the scene.
See if you can find it **7** times!

Trace and write the number **7**.

• 8 • Lily can really jump rope! Jump faster Lily!

1-2-3 Count and circle **8** jump ropes.

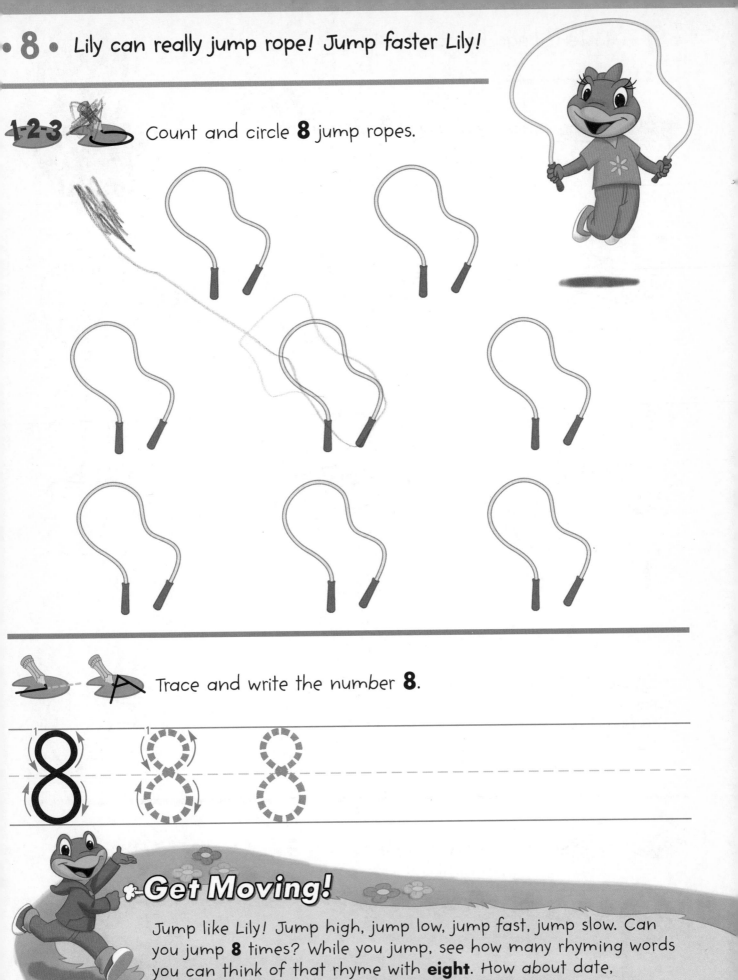

Trace and write the number **8**.

8   8   8

✿ Get Moving!

Jump like Lily! Jump high, jump low, jump fast, jump slow. Can you jump **8** times? While you jump, see how many rhyming words you can think of that rhyme with **eight**. How about date, plate, state, great! What else can you do with the number **8**?

Listen! Leap has a whistle.

 Count and color **9** whistles.

  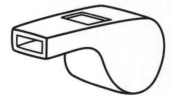

  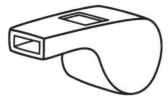

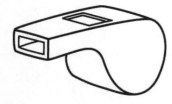  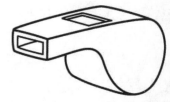

  Trace and write the number **9**.

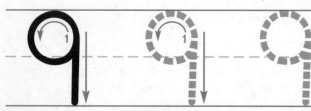

Lily loves to read.
What will her story be about?

 Count and color **10** books that you think Lily would like to read next.

  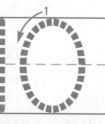 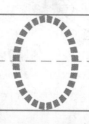 

  Trace and write the number **10**.

10 10 10

• 1-10 •

Lily carries her books in her backpack.
That's heavy!
What else does she have in there?

Draw a line to connect the dots in order from **1** to **10** to find out what else Lily has in her backpack.
Then, color the picture.

⚡Get Moving!

How many things can you carry?
Can you carry **1** book, **2** soup cans, **4** toys, **6** shoes, **9** t-shirts or **10** stuffed animals? What else can you carry? Bend over and see if you can keep a stuffed animal on your back while you walk **10** steps. Don't forget to balance!

 Count and color **11** airplanes.

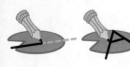 Trace and write the number **11**.

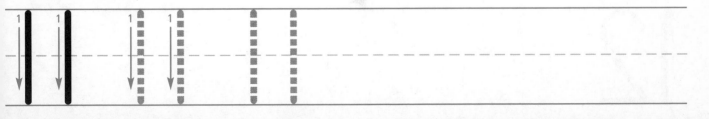

• 12 •

Hey, batter batter!
Leap and Lily are playing baseball.

 Draw lines from **12** baseballs to the baseball mitt.

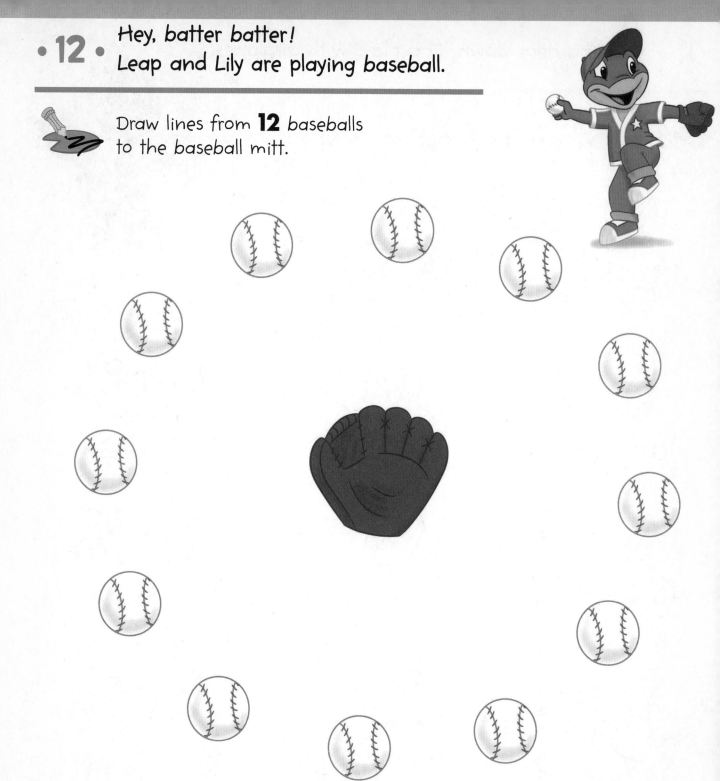

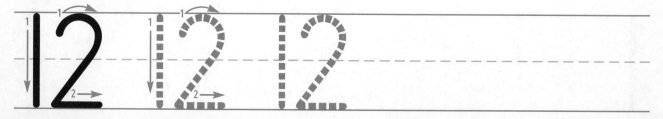 Trace and write the number **12**.

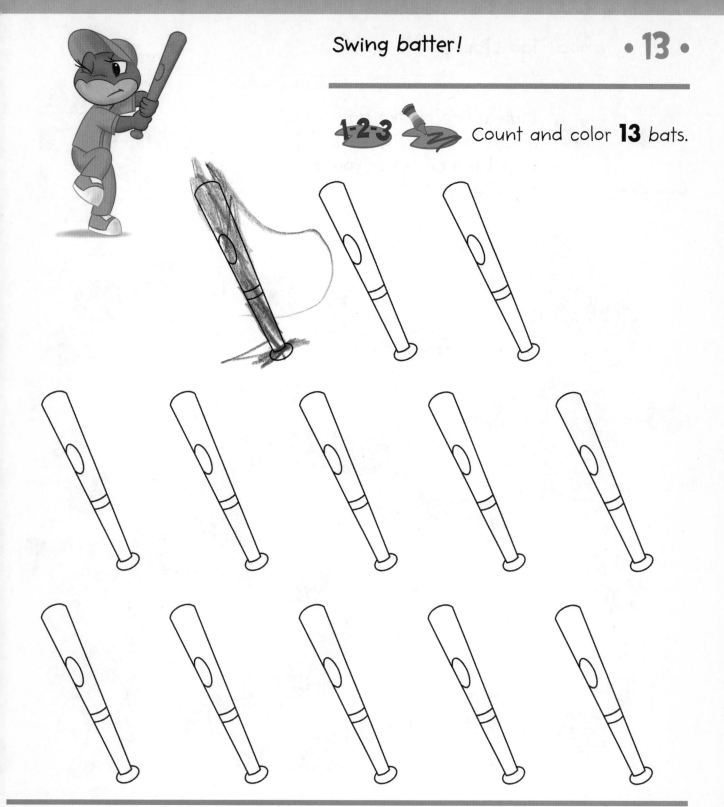

1-2-3 Count and color **13** bats.

Trace and write the number **13**.

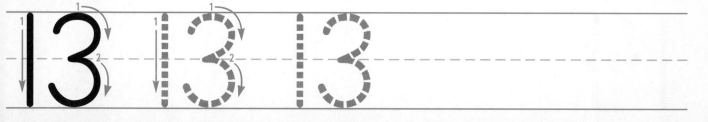

 **14** • Whoa! Tad stacked **14** blocks.

Draw a line on the path of blocks in order from **1** to **14**. Count the blocks as you go from Tad to Dot.

 Trace and write the number **14**.

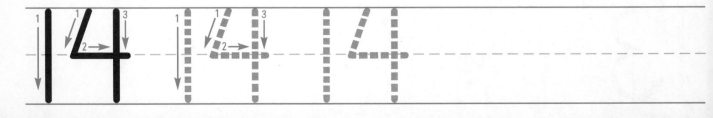

Nibble nibble. Lily is feeding the rabbits.

 Count and circle **15** rabbits.
Then, draw **15** carrots –
one for each rabbit you circled.

  Trace and write the number **15**.

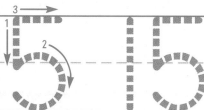

Get Moving!

Hop like a rabbit and count your
steps from **1** to **15**! Try different kinds of animal moves. You can
try chipmunk steps, frog leaps, kangaroo jumps, horse gallops
or elephant stomps. What other animal steps can you try?
Try them **15** times each!

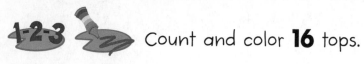 Count and color **16** tops.

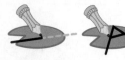 Trace and write the number **16**.

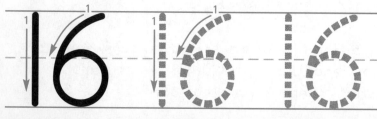

Roar! Leap has **17** very loud dinosaurs.

 Count and circle **17** of Leap's favorite dinosaurs.

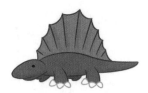

  Trace and write the number **17**.

17 17 17

Lily is drawing. Tad is coloring.

 Draw **18** spots on Lily's butterfly. Then, color the picture.

  Trace and write the number **18**.

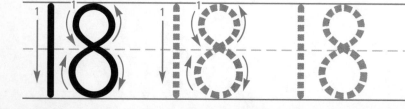

Color **19** circles to help Tad color his caterpillar.

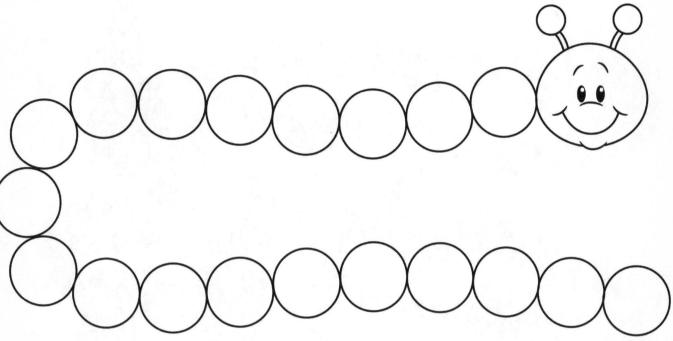

  Trace and write the number **19**.

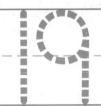

Get Moving!

Do the caterpillar *boogie!* Try to walk on all fours (two hands and two feet). Can you take **19** steps? Try flying like a butterfly, too. Don't forget to flap your beautiful wings **19** times.

Vanilla - mmm!
That's Leap's favorite ice cream flavor!

 Count and color **20** stones
on the path that will take
Leap to the ice cream shop.

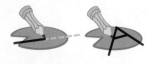 Trace and write the number **20**.

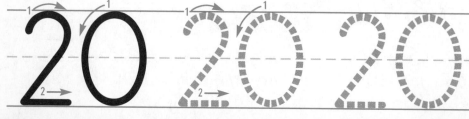

• 1-20 •

That's yummy!
Leap, Lily and Tad love cool treats!

 Draw a line to connect the dots from **1** to **20** to find a cool treat that Lily likes. Then, color the picture.

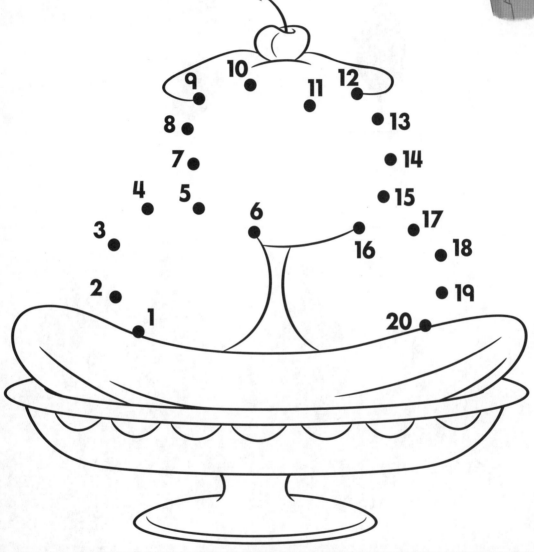

 Draw a picture to show how many cherries you would like on your sundae. Then, count your cherries and write the number.

Leap, Lily and Tad are hopping and jumping on their way home.

Find the pictures in the scene below. Then, count and write the number to show how many you found.

You are a super counter!

Pre K Math

- Counting
- Writing Numbers
- Shapes
- Sizes
- Physical Activity

Pre K Math Parent Tips

Sort by Size

Review the various size words with your child, like **small**, **medium**, **large** or **big**, **short**, **tall**, **long**, and **short**. Then, have your child arrange his or her toys by size. For example, if your child has several toy animals, you might ask, "Which animal is **big** and which animal is **small**?" or "Can you find an animal that is **bigger** than the monkey?" You can also place toys in a size pattern and help your child complete the pattern. You might start by alternating **big** and **small** toys, or **long** and **short** toys. Can your child find something that would come next in the pattern?

Get Moving! Tall and Short

Explain to your child that you are going to play a game of **tall** and **short** by saying a word or showing a picture of an object, animal, or person. If your child thinks that the picture shows something **tall**, then he or she must stretch to try and touch the sky. If your child thinks that the picture shows something **short**, then he or she must crouch down low to the ground. You can use photos from a magazine or family album to have your child guess about who is **taller** and who is **shorter** in the pictures. You may want to start with the following **tall** and **short** words: a giraffe, a building, a mouse, a cat, a tree, a light post, a street sign, a bug, a snake, a roller coaster.

Search for Shapes

Play "I Spy" with shapes. Have your child look outside for something that is in the shape of a **square**, or in the kitchen for something that is shaped like a **triangle**. Count the sides on each of the shapes you find to reinforce the learning. Look for shapes as you walk in the neighborhood or in a store. Encourage your child to come up with shapes for you to look for, too! Shapes are everywhere – what shapes can you find?

Shape Art

Cut out various colored shapes from construction paper to make a shape collage. Try making a picture of a house with a **square** and a **triangle**. Or, make a car with **rectangles** and **circles**. What other shape pictures can you make? Be creative and use different sizes and colors! For a variation, you can cut shapes out of a material like felt and arrange the shapes on top of each other (they will stick without glue!). Try using colorful pipe cleaners to make shapes, too.

Remember the Number

Play a game with numbers and number words. Cut out ten small squares of paper. Use five of the squares and write the numbers **1** through **5**, one on each square of paper. On the other five squares, write the number words **one** through **five**. Place all of the squares of paper facing down on a table and mix them up. Have your child flip over two cards at a time and try to match each number with its number word. When your child is ready, add the numbers and the number words up to ten or higher.

Leap is excited to play baseball!

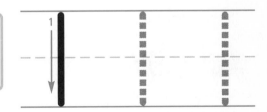

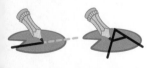 **1-2-3**

Count and color **1** baseball.

Trace and write the number **1**.

1

Leap and Tad are playing catch.

 Count and color **2** baseball mitts and **2** baseball hats.

 Circle the group with **2**.

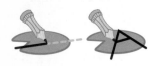 Trace and write the number **2**.

Tad and Leap are on the green team.
Lily is on the blue team.

 Count and circle the players on the blue team.

      Color **3** water bottles.

  Trace and write the number **3**.

Lily dumped a bucket of softballs on the field.

Count and circle **4** yellow balls.

Color **4** baseball gloves.

 Trace and write the number **4**.

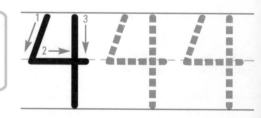

The green team is ready to play ball!

 Count and circle **5** players on the green team.

 Draw an X on the group that shows **5**.

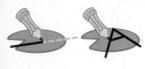 Trace and write the number **5**.

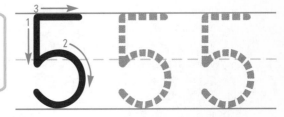

There are so many things to count at the ballpark.

  Count the objects in the picture below and write the number that shows how many next to each picture.

 _____

 _____

 _____

 _____

Look at all the fans who have come to watch the game.

1-2-3  Count and circle **6** fans.

Trace and write the number **6**.

⚡Get Moving!

Count to **6** while you jog like Leap. Try doing some other warm-up activities that you know. Do them **6** times!

It's the 7th inning stretch! Snack time!

 Count and color **7** boxes of popcorn.

 Draw an X on the group that shows **7**.

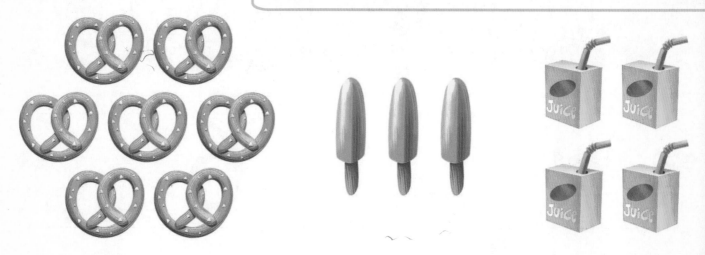

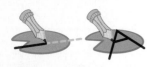 Trace and write the number **7**.

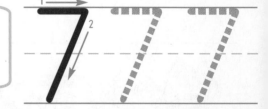

There are **8** birds on the field.

 Count and circle **8** birds.

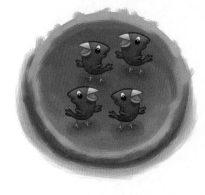 Circle the group with **8**.

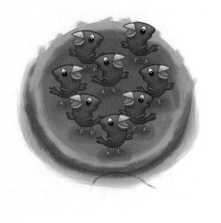
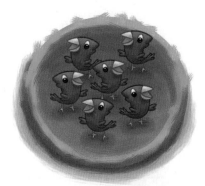

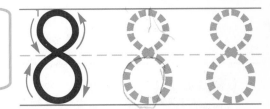 Trace and write the number **8**.

Tad hit the ball into the trees!

Count and circle **9** trees.

Count and color **9** leaves.

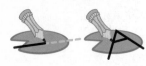

Trace and write the number **9**.

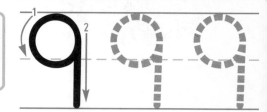

✶Get Moving!

Count the trees in your yard and write how many. _____
See if you can find **9** leaves in your yard. Can you find **9** small sticks?
See if you can find the number **9** in your house somewhere.

• Counting to nine • Identifying the number 9 • Physical activity

Lily sees a soccer team warming up!

 Count and circle **10** soccer shoes.

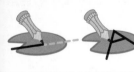 Trace and write the number **10**.

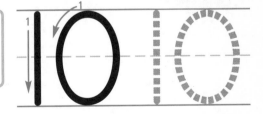

A soccer ball is shaped like a **circle**.
A **circle** is round.

 Trace the **circles**.
Then, draw more of your own.

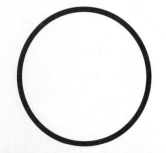 Great Job!

 Color the **circles**.

  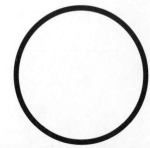

• Identifying circles • Tracing and drawing circles

When Tad plays soccer, his jersey has a **square** on it.
A **square** has four sides that are all the same.

 Trace the **squares**.
Then, draw more of your own.

 Draw an X on the **squares**.

Lily's soccer bag has a **triangle** on it.
A **triangle** has three sides and three corners.

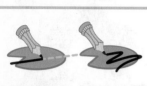

Trace the **triangles**.
Then, draw more of your own.

Color the **triangles**.

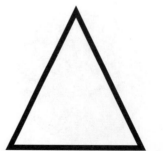

A **rectangle** has four sides.
Two sides are short and two sides are long.

The soccer team's photo is in the shape of a **rectangle**.

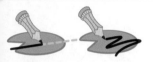

Trace the **rectangles**.
Then, draw more of your own.

 Color the **rectangles**.

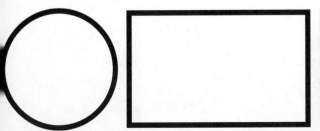

Leap, Lily, and Tad love to play soccer!

Can you find all the shapes in the picture?
Draw an X on any **circles**, **squares**,
triangles or **rectangles**.

Draw a line from **1-10** to see a healthy snack that is good to eat during a game – it will give you energy! Color the snack.

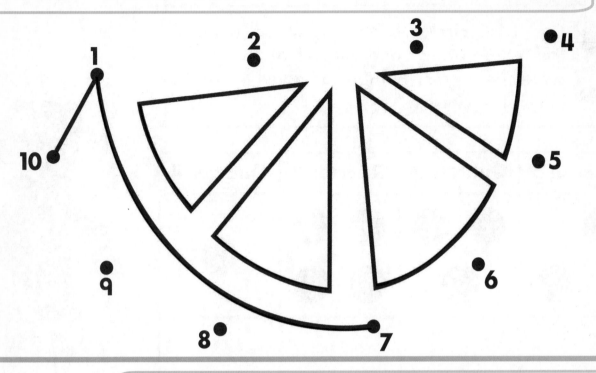

Draw a line from **1-10** to see something that players need when they are thirsty! Color the picture.

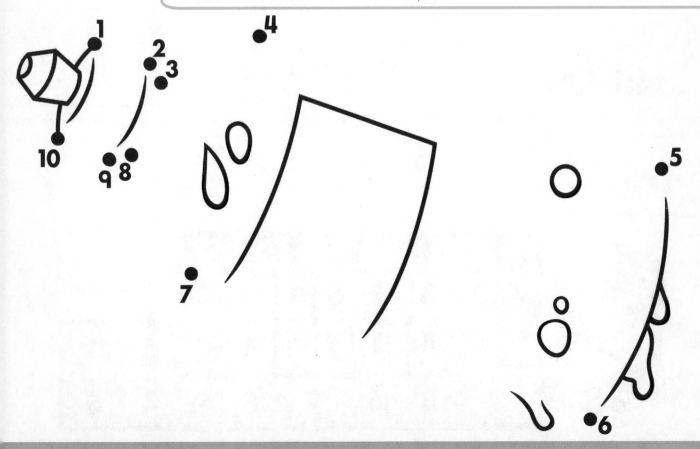

Leap draws a **circle** for each goal his team scores.

Count the **circles** to show how many goals the team had in each quarter of the game. Write the correct number of goals in the box below the **circles**.

Quarter 1	Quarter 2	Quarter 3	Quarter 4
● ●	● ● ●	● ● ● ●	●

Now, count all of the **circles** together. Write how many. _____

Draw a line from **1-10**, to help Tad find the right path to the goal.

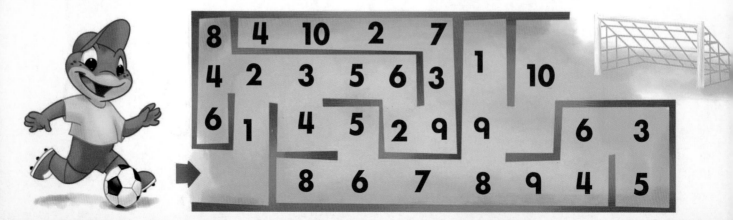

● Number order ● One to one correspondence ● Writing numbers ● Counting to ten

The teams are warming up before the big game!

Look at the order of the warm-ups. First, next, and last .

 Draw a line from a number to each picture to show what the players did first, next, and last.

 Circle the picture that comes first. Put an X on the picture that comes last.

1

2

3

☘ Get Moving!

See if you can do the warm-ups in the same order as the players.
Try it! Now, try 3 warm-ups of your own!

Leap wants to try football now.
Help the players find the helmet that fits.

 Draw a line to match the size of the helmet to the size of the player's head—**small**, **medium**, or **large**.

 Circle the **biggest** head.
Draw an X on the **smallest** head.

The **tallest** player is the quarterback,
the **medium-sized** player is the defender, and the
shortest player is the kicker.

 Draw a line from the player to the referee that is the same height.

 Color the **tallest** item in each group.

The fans are hungry!

 Draw a line to match the size of the snack to the size of the fan.

Draw a path to help Professor Quigley find a snack by following the pattern – **small, large, small, large**.

START

FINISH

Football players need to stretch so they don't get hurt!

First, Tad stands on his tiptoes and tries to reach the sky.

Next, Tad jumps up and down.

Last, Tad taps his feet in a little dance.

 Write 1, 2, or 3 below each picture to show the correct order.

_____

_____

_____

Get Moving!

Can you try these stretches too? Now try some new stretches – start stretching with your head and work your way down to your toes.

 Look at the **patterns**. Circle what comes next.

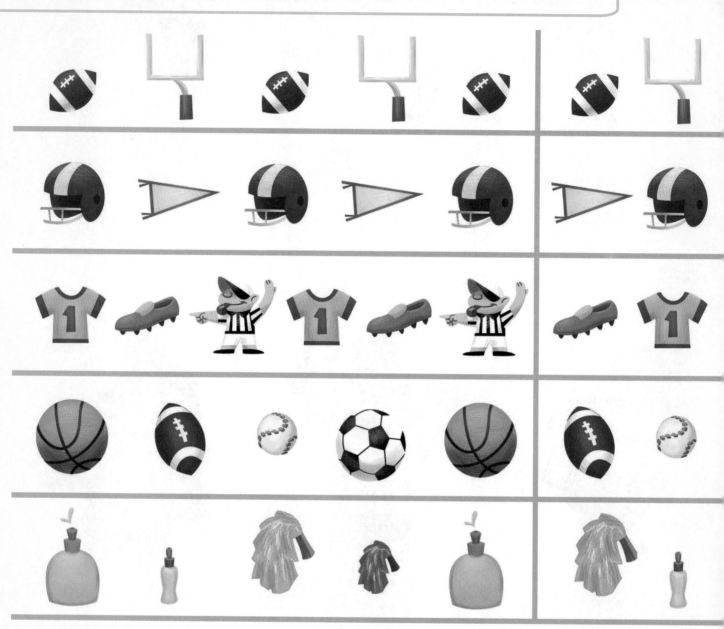

 Now, draw your own **pattern**.

• Identifying patterns • Completing patterns • Creativity

 Look at the **patterns**. Draw what comes next.

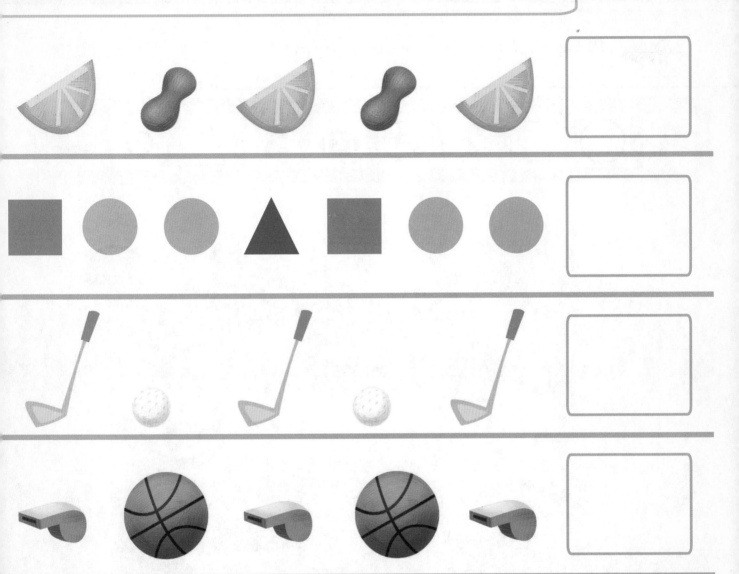

 Draw a **pattern** of your favorite foods!

Find the hidden items in the picture.

 Draw an X on the items as you find them.

9 ◯ ▢ **2**  🏈 **3** △ ◯ 🐛

 Circle each player on the green team. Draw an X on each player on the blue team. Draw a square around each fan who is cheering for the players.

 Write the answers on the lines.

How many **triangles** can you find in the picture? _____

How many **squares**? _____

How many **circles**? _____

Write the numbers that you see in the picture.

_____

Time to celebrate after the big game! Color the spaces using the color code to discover the hidden picture.

1 = ● 2 = ● 3 = ● 4 = ● 5 = ● 6 = ●

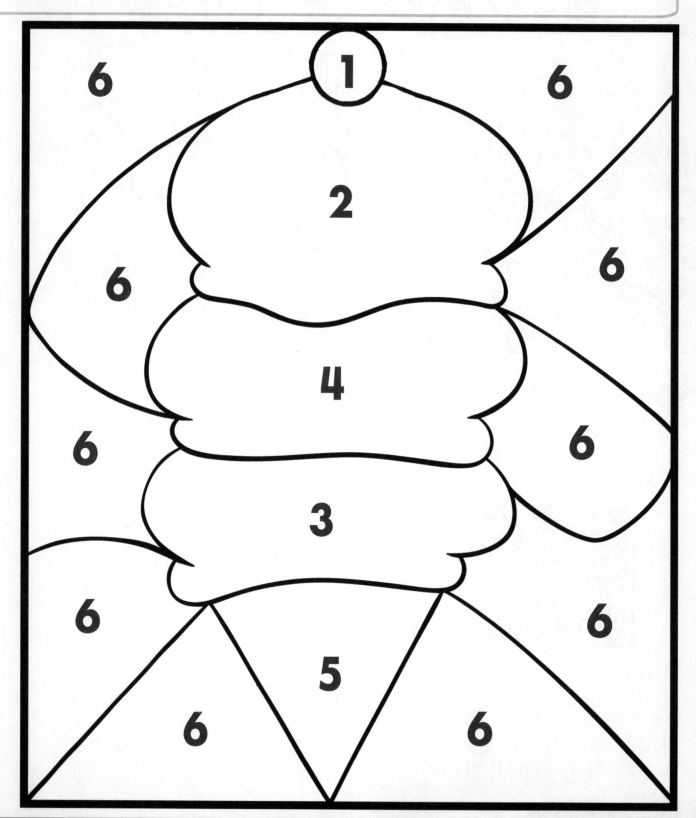

• Identifying colors • Matching

Look at the number line at the top of the page.

Write a **3** on the shirt.
Write a **10** on the paper.
Write a **7** on the cup.
Write a **9** on the hat.
Write a **2** on the popcorn bag.

 Practice writing the numbers **1-10**.

Follow the numbers from **1-10** to help
Lily get home after the game.

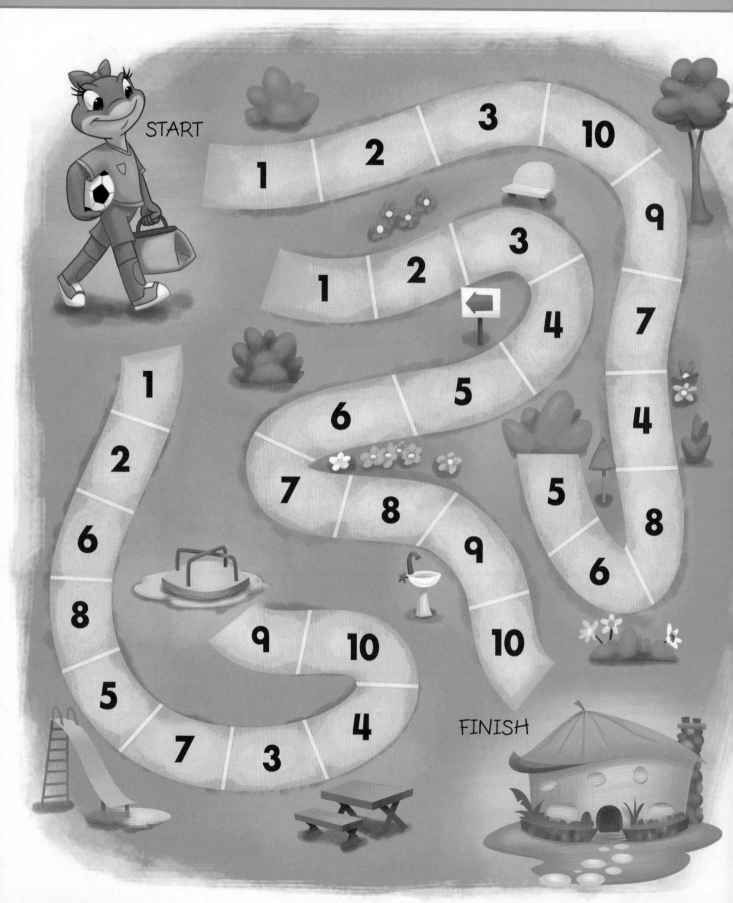

START

FINISH

• Identifying numbers • Number order

The game is over! Good game!

 Circle the group with more circles to show the winner!

 Count the fans who are cheering. Write the number on the line.

 Count all the players that you see. Write the number on the line.

Draw an X on the items in the box as you find them in the picture.

1-2-3

Count the friends in the picture.
Find the hidden numbers **7** and **3**.
Circle the **triangles**.
Draw an X on the **squares**.

Pre K Reading and Writing

- **Letter Recognition**
- **Beginning Letter Sounds**
- **Beginning Writing**
- **Physical Activity**
- **Creativity**

Pre K Reading and Writing Parent Tips

Get Moving! Letter Hopscotch

Find a rock for a marker, and draw a hopscotch board on the sidewalk or driveway. For this game, you will write a letter inside each square instead of numbers. You may want to use the following letters to *begin*: **t**, **r**, **s**, **b**, **n**, **p**, **l**, **w**, **d**, and **g**. Play the game as you would play hopscotch, *but* when the rock lands on a letter square, your child must name a word that *begins* with that letter sound in order to advance to the next letter. Take turns, and the first player who identifies a word for each letter sound is the winner!

Get Moving! Letter Dance

Clear a safe place inside to move around, or find a space outside to try this silly letter dance. Do an action dance with your child for each letter of the alphabet. For example, you might **a**ct silly, **b**ounce, **c**artwheel, or **d**ance...try to act out all of the letters with different movements! Encourage your child to think of actions, and *be* sure to emphasize the beginning letter sound for each word.

Tasty Letters

Have fun making letter snacks with your child. Can you form the letter **c** with carrot slices, a **b** with *blueberries*, or a **p** with pretzel sticks? Try making letters out of *bread* dough or cookie dough: you can cook the dough for a fresh and tasty letter treat! Or, try some alphabet soup or cereal with your child and spoon up different letters. Tell your child you are hungry for a **t** or a **d**. See if you can find the whole alphabet!

Sticky Letter Partners

Use a large sticky note pad and a small sticky note pad. On a large piece of sticky paper, write an uppercase letter. Encourage your child to use the small sticky paper to write the appropriate lowercase letter partner. Make a few pairs, mix up the partners, and see if your child can match them correctly. When a correct match is made, stick the partners together! For a variation, use regular paper and tape, or glue the letter partners together when you make a match.

Sock It to Me!

Find a *bunch* of clean socks and play this silly **s** sound game with your child. You sit at one end of the room and give your child a stack of socks at the other end of the room. Encourage your child to think of a word that *begins* with the sound of **s**. When an **s** word is identified, he or she may roll up a sock and throw it at you! If your child cannot think of an **s** word, you can help with clues or prompting, or you may throw a sock at your child! Change the letter and play again.

Join Leap and his family for a day at the circus!

 Draw a line to match the letter partners.

A

c

a

B

b

C

d

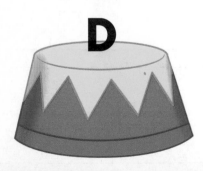

D

WOW!
Watch the acrobat do flips!

Color the pictures that begin with the sound of **Aa** like acrobat.

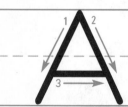

Trace and write the letter **A** and **a**.

A A A

a a a

It's fun to watch the bears!

 Draw a line to connect each bear to a picture inside the ball that begins with the sound of **Bb**.

 Trace and write the letter **B** and **b**.

B B B

b b b

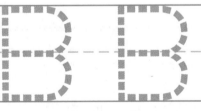 **Get Moving!**

Grab a ball and see if you can balance it on your head like a circus bear! What else can you do with a ball?

Who performs silly circus acts?

 Say the name of each picture.
Color the spaces that have pictures
that begin with the sound of **Cc**.

 Trace and write the letter **C** and **c**.

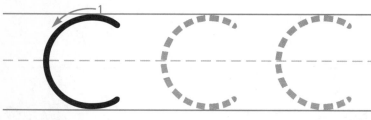

Tad loves dessert!

 Circle the dog if the picture on its outfit begins with the sound of **Dd**.

 Trace and write the letter **D** and **d**.

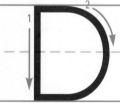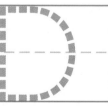 D D D

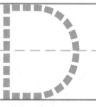 d d d

Those balloons are so colorful!

Write the letter partner.
Color the balloons.

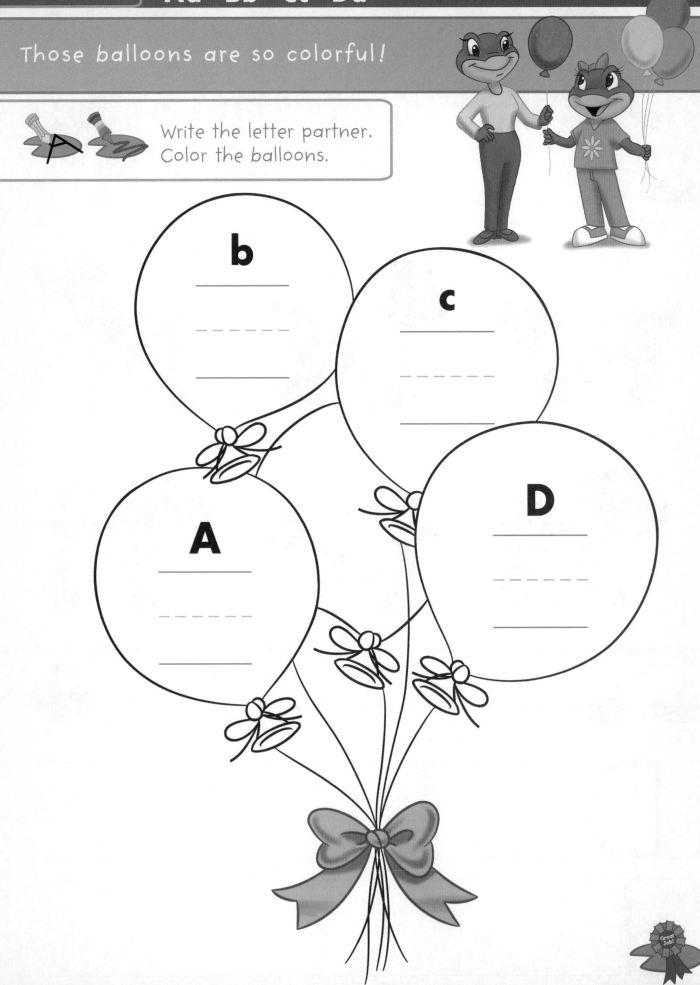

b

c

A

D

• Letter recognition • Beginning sounds • Recognizing letter partners

Everyone loves the elephants!

Find and circle the objects that start with the sound of **Ee**. Color the elephant if he is wearing letter partners.

Ea

Bb

Aa

Ce

Ee

EXIT

Dd

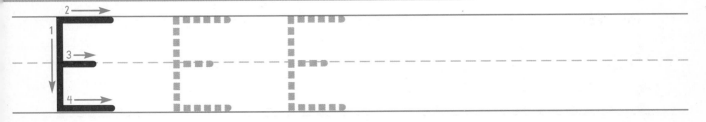

Trace and write the letter **E** and **e**.

2 →
1 ↓
3 →
4 →

E

é²
1→

e e

Help the flying trapeze artist get the flag.

 Draw a line to follow the path with the pictures whose names begin with the **Ff** sound.

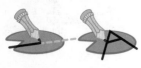 Trace and write the letter **F** and **f**.

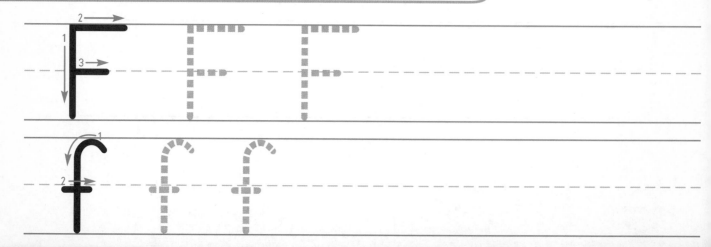

Lily sees some things that begin with **Gg**, do you?

 Circle the hidden pictures that begin with the **Gg** sound.

 ghost goat gorilla  guitar gate

  Trace and write the letter **G** and **g**.

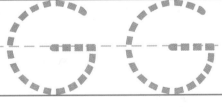

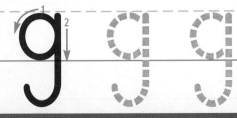

A circus horse can gallop quickly!

 Color the horses that are wearing a picture that begins with the **Hh** sound.

 Trace and write the letter **H** and **h**.

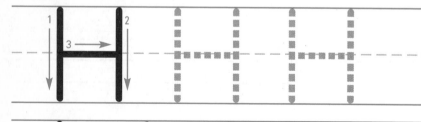

The Ringmaster needs your help to match letter partners.

 Draw a line to match the letter partners.

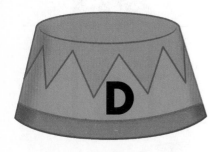 **D**

 **f**

 **E**

 **h**

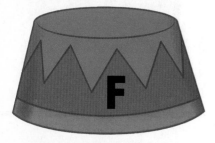 **F**

 **d**

 **G**

 **e**

 **H**

 **g**

This circus is so interesting!

 Trace the **i** to complete each word.

inch

ink

itch

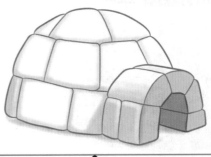

insect

igloo

  Trace and write the letter **I** and **i**.

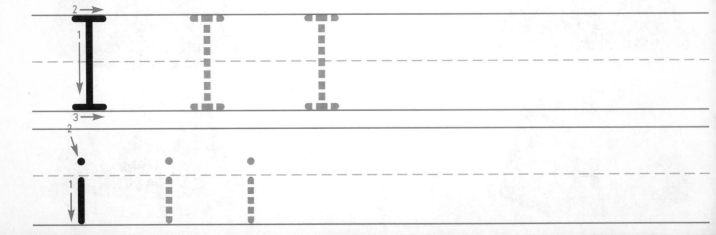

Wow! The juggler can juggle things that begin with **Jj**.

 Circle the balls that have a picture beginning with the **Jj** sound.

Trace and write the letter **J** and **j**.

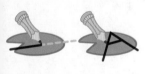

J J J J

j j j j

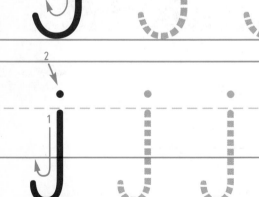

Get Moving!

Do 10 jumping jacks. Now jump as high as you can. Can you jiggle? What else can you do that begins with the letter **Jj**?

Time for more tricks!
The Ringmaster is opening the lion cage with a big key.

 Write **k** or **l** to complete each word.

_____ angaroo

_____ adybug

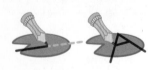 Trace and write the letter **K** and **k**.

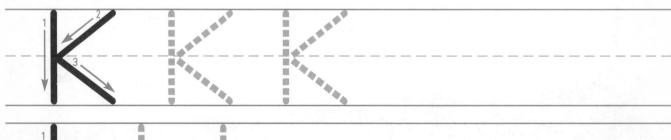

• Tracing and writing the letter Kk • Letter recognition • Beginning sounds

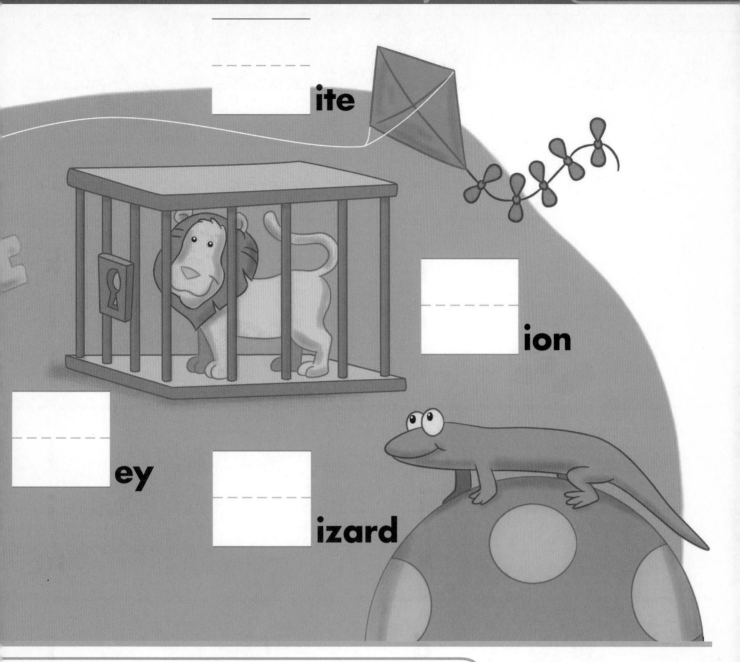

___ite

___ion

___ey

___izard

 Trace and write the letter **L** and **l**.

Help Lily find the beginning sound for each picture.

 Circle the letter you hear at the beginning of each picture name.

j
i
l

k
l
j

b
j
k

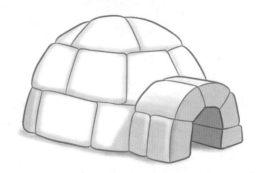

l
i
m

d
l
h

j
i
k

  What letter sound does the name Lily begin with? Circle the letter partners that make the sound.

Kk   **Ii**   **Jj**   **Ll**   **Aa**

• Letter recognition • Beginning sounds

Here comes the **Mm** band!

 Draw a line to connect each marcher with a picture that begins with the **Mm** sound.

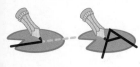 Trace and write the letter **M** and **m**.

M M M

m m m

✴ Get Moving!

Get up and march! Sing the alphabet letters as you march around the room. March fast, march slow, march high, march low! Make up your own marching song.

What number word begins with the sound of **Nn**?

Use **blue** to color each space that has a picture whose name begins with the **Nn** sound. Color the other picture spaces **red**.

 Trace and write the letter **N** and **n**.

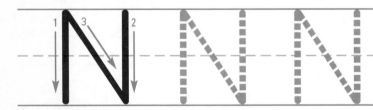

Oh boy, Leap and Grandpa
are having fun!

 Trace the **o** to complete each word.

o x

octopus

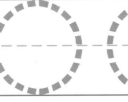

ostrich

olive

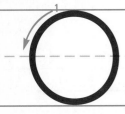 Trace and write the letter **O** and **o**.

O O O

o o o

The elephants love to eat peanuts.

 Color the peanuts whose picture begins with the **Pp** sound.

 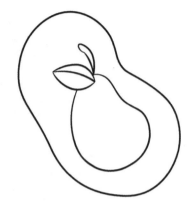 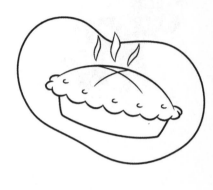

  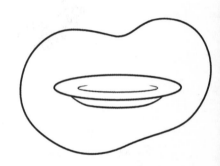

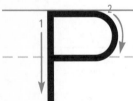 Trace and write the letter **P** and **p**.

P P P P

p p p p

• Tracing and writing the letter Pp • Letter recognition • Beginning sounds

Help the clowns say the sounds of each letter they are holding.

Circle the letter you hear at the beginning of each picture name.

p
o
n

n
p
m

m
p
o

p
o
n

o
m
p

m
n
p

Look! Tad found a shiny quarter!

 Trace the **q** to complete each word.

quilt

queen

  Trace and write the letter **Q** and **q**.

Q Q Q Q

q q q q

• Tracing and writing the letter Qq • Letter recognition • Beginning sounds

Oh no! The lion will not get back in his cage.

 Help the Ringmaster catch the lion by drawing a line on the path of pictures that begin with **Rr**.

START

FINISH

Trace and write the letter **R** and **r**.

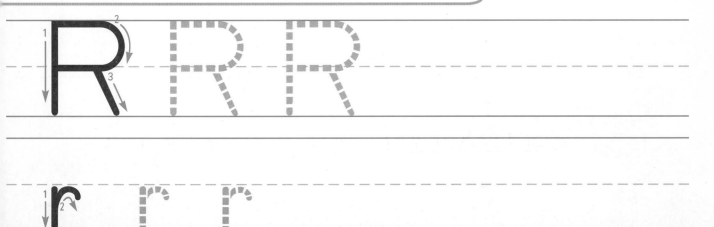

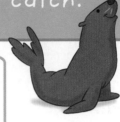

Seals are really good at playing catch.

Draw a line from each seal to a ball with a picture that begins with the **Ss** sound.

Trace and write the letter **S** and **s**.

S S S

s s s

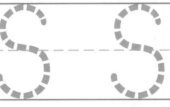

Get Moving!

Can you balance a soccer ball on your nose like a seal?
Try other **S** actions like stretching, skipping, and making silly faces!
What other things can you do that begin with **s**?

Tiger tamers are so brave!

 Color the pictures that begin with the **Tt** sound.

  Trace and write the letter **T** and **t**.

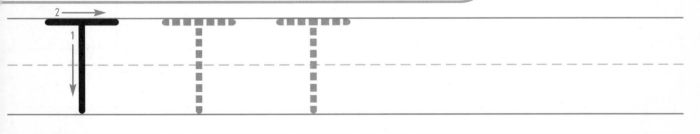

Let's play Tic-Tac-Toe!

Color the row that has three pictures that all begin with the same sound.

• Letter recognition • Beginning sounds

Look at those clowns!

 Trace the **u** and **v** to complete each word.

volcano

up

violets

umpire

umbrella

vase

Oh no! The clown is squirting
Leap and Lily with water!

 Color the pictures that begin
with the **Ww** sound.

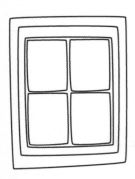

  Trace and write the letter **W** and **w**.

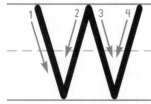

W W W W

W W W

• Tracing and writing the letter Ww • Letter recognition • Beginning sounds

Here comes **x**, **y** and **z**!

 Trace the letter that completes each word.

zebra

exit

yarn

zipper

x-ray

yellow

Help find the hidden letters.

  These letters are hiding under the big tent: **u**, **v**, **w**, **x**, **y**, and **z**. Find and circle them.

• Letter recognition • Visual discrimination

The circus is a lot of fun!

Circle the letter you hear at the beginning of each picture name.

k
m
j

t
z
c

p
r
w

n
h
f

b
c
s

p
e
l

r
n
q

y
s
d

b
p
r

Get Moving!

See if you can try an action for all of the letters in your name.
This is what Tad can do: **T**-tip toe, **A**-act like an alligator, **D**-dance!
What actions can you do?

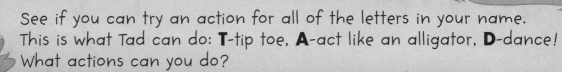

Write the missing letter partners.

A a   C c

D d   E e

G g   I i   J j

Ll M m

O o   Q q   R r

T t   U u

W w   Y y

• Writing letters • Letter recognition

Write On!

- Drawing Lines
- Drawing Shapes
- Tracing Letters
- Writing Letters
- Letter Partners

Write On! Parent Tips

The Scribble Game

Play a drawing scribble game with your child to get loosened up and ready to write. Start with a simple shape or squiggle line and ask your child to make a picture out of it by adding more lines, shapes, or colors. Ask your child if the scribble looks like any of the letters of the alphabet. Talk about the curves and lines that you see in the scribble. Or, practice scribbling in large zigzags and curves to get ready to print letters.

Powdery Letters

Try a tactile or hands-on approach to learning about the shapes and lines that make up letters. Spread salt, sugar, or flour on a cookie sheet and let your child write letters in the powder with his or her finger. Erase the lines and try a new letter. Or, try writing letters in the sand or sandbox with a stick. Sandpaper letters are fun to touch and feel too!

Get Moving! Running in Circles

Find an open space to move and run outside. Encourage your child to run or walk in different shapes and lines. You may want to start by asking your child to run in a straight line to a tree, walk in zigzags like an alligator, or run in circles like a spinning top or the letter O. When you think your child is ready, try making a path that looks like a letter!

Get Moving! Letter Babies

Draw an uppercase letter on the ground outside with chalk, and draw a few lowercase letters around it. Have your child stand on the uppercase letter in the middle and then encourage him or her to jump to the matching letter partner. Or, write the uppercase letters in one row and the matching lowercase letter partners (mixed-up) in another row. Your child can jump from row to row in order to find matching letter partners.

Name Mobile

As children enter school, they are asked to recognize and write their own names. You can help encourage name recognition at home by making a name mobile with your child. Help your child to cut out colorful construction paper letters that spell his or her name. Attach them to a hanger with string and help your child decorate the mobile with special photos, pictures of favorite things, feathers, string, ribbons, or other colorful craft items. Hang the mobile in your child's room and watch it spin.

Work Those Fingers!

Children who are learning to write need extra practice in fine motor control and eye-hand coordination. Activities like lacing cards with string, manipulating play dough, and stringing beads can help build strong finger muscles that are needed for controlling crayons and pencils. You can also allow your child to scribble on old newspaper, button buttons, snap snaps, tear paper, and make up finger plays to move, exercise, and work those fingers!

Leap, Lily, and Tad want
to go bike riding. Let's ride!

Trace the **straight** lines from
each friend to his or her bike.

Leap, Lily, and Tad ride their bikes downhill. Wheeeeeeeeeee!

 Trace the **diagonal** lines for each path.

Now, Leap wants to play basketball.
That ball really bounces!

 Trace the **zig zag** lines for the bouncing balls.

☀Get Moving!

Run on different shaped paths. Run on a straight path, run on a curvy path, then try some zig zags. Flap your arms and make noises as you go! What other kinds of paths can you try?

Tad pretends he is sailing.
Look at that boat move! Ahoy!

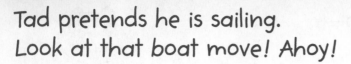

Trace the **wavy** lines of the boat paths.

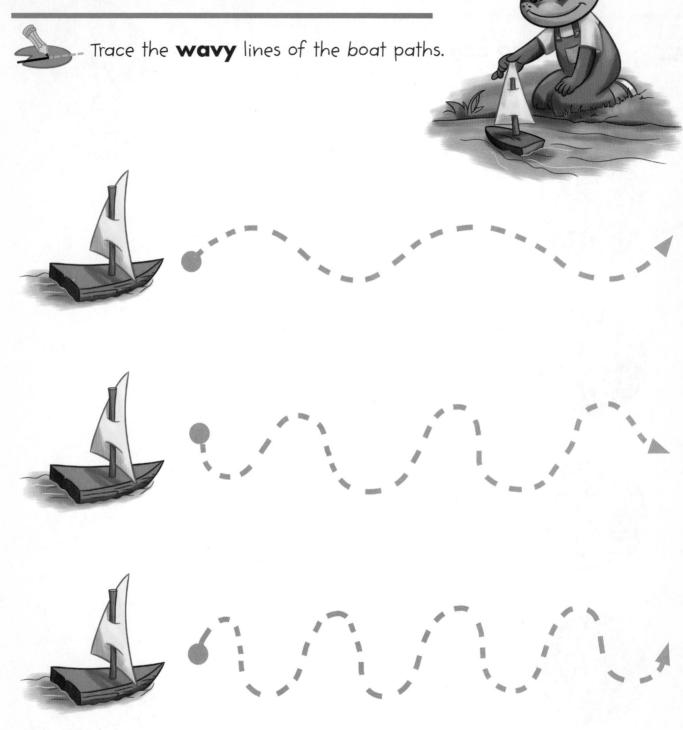

Lily likes drawing beautiful flowers.

 Trace the **loopy** lines on the petals of the flower. Then, color it.

Look! Tad is flying his toy plane.

Trace the **curly** lines for the path of each plane.

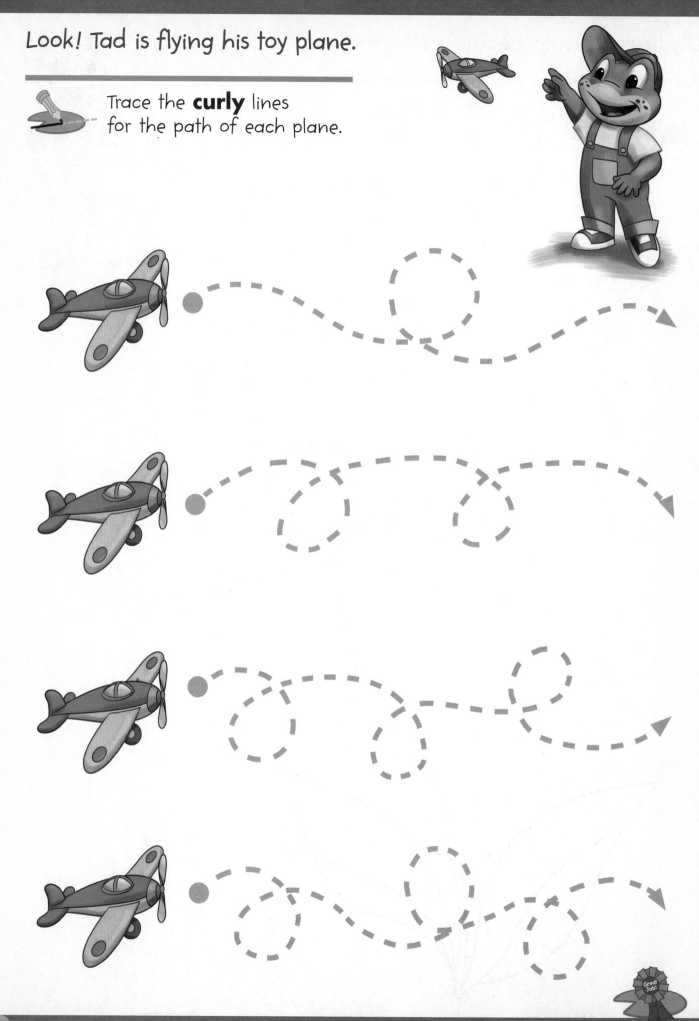

Leap wants to go roller skating. Which path should he take?

 Draw a line to help Leap get to the skate park.

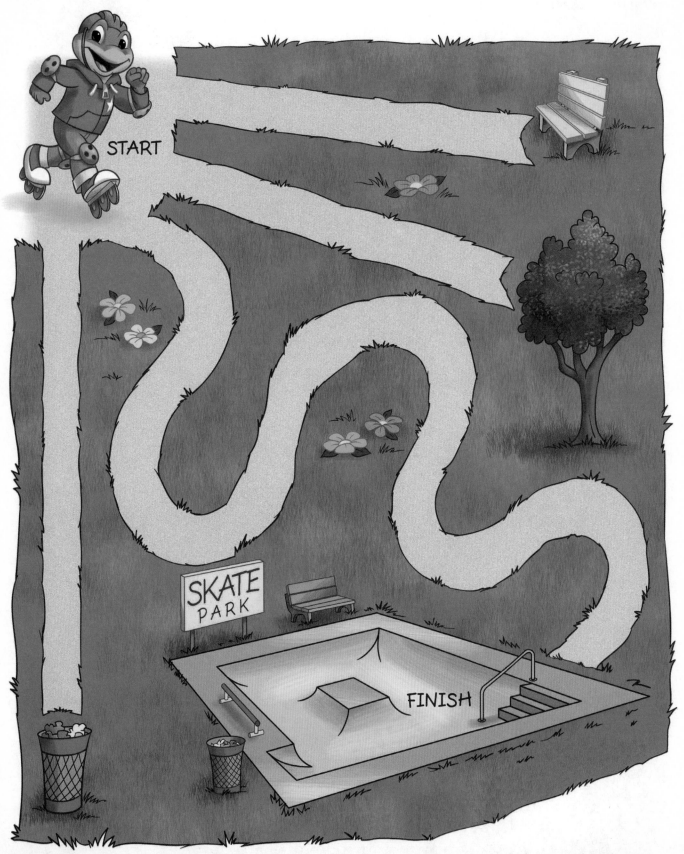

Tad has fun playing with blocks.
Look at all the shapes!

 Trace the **shapes**.
Then, color them.

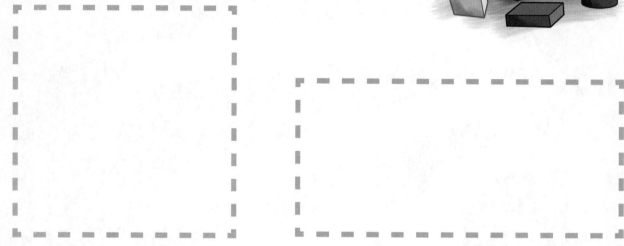

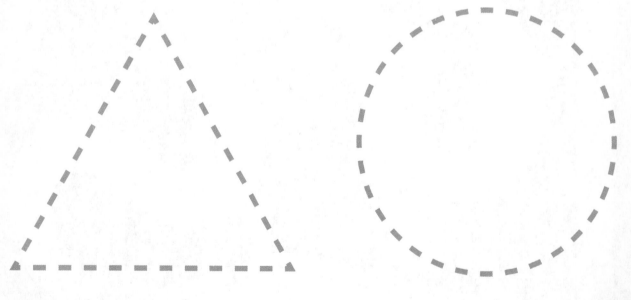

Get Moving!

Make some giant shapes with sidewalk chalk on your driveway.
See if you can tip toe along the path of the shapes. Can you
slide, walk backwards, or hop on the path too? What else can
you do to move on the path of the shapes?

Leap made a pattern with Tad's blocks.

Draw the shape at the end of each row that continues the pattern. Then, color the shapes.

Lily drew some shape patterns.

 Look at the pattern in each row. Draw and color what comes next.

 Draw and color your own shape pattern.

What a mess! Help Leap clean up his room.

Draw a **circle** around nine things that are out of place. Then, draw a **straight** line to where they really belong.

Get Moving!

Play Circle and Straight. Find a ball for each player. Throw the ball and when it stops rolling, each player must run straight to his or her ball, run around it in a circle, and then run straight back to the starting spot. Play again with new rules!

10, 9, 8, 7, 6, 5, 4, 3, 2, 1 – Blast off!
Tad pretends to take a trip to the stars.

Trace the lines to finish the picture. Then, color it.

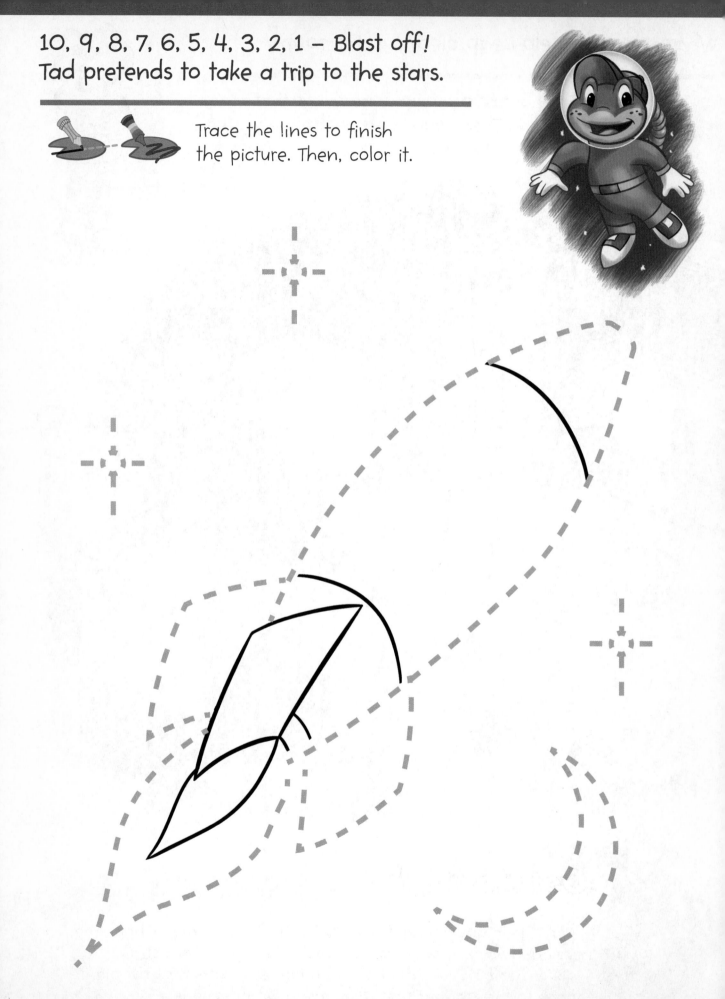

Lily loves lollipops!

 Draw a path to the center of the lollipop without touching the purple swirl.

START

FINISH

Lily practices writing letters in her little green notebook. Now it's your turn!

Trace the **uppercase letters**. Then, write some of your own.

A B C

D E

F G H

I J K

L M

Get Moving!

See if you can make your body into the shape of letters of the alphabet. Start with the letter **T** or **I** or **L**. You can try sitting, standing, bending, or squatting. What other letters can you make? Find a partner and see if you can make a **K** or a **W** together. Try the other letters too!

Leap and Tad play baseball together.

Trace the **uppercase letters** on the baseball diamond. Then, draw a **straight** line on the path from H-O-M-E to help Leap score a home run!

Lovely letters, Lily!

Draw a line to connect the dots from **uppercase** **A** to **Z** to see what Lily is doing. Then, color the picture.

Hmmmm. Lily sees some small letters.
Small letters are called lowercase.

Trace the **lowercase letters** that you see. Then, write some of your own.

a   b   c

d   e   f

g   h   i

j   k   l

m   n   o

p   q   r

s   t   u

v   w   x

y   z

Great Job!

Leap is skateboarding.
He wants to skateboard to the ice cream shop.

Draw a line on the path of only **lowercase letters** to help him get there.

Tad is chasing something.

Connect the dots from **lowercase a** to **z** to find out what it is. Then, color the picture.

d• c• b• y• •x
e• •a z• •w
f• •v
g• •u
h• •t
i• •s
j• n o •r
•m
k• •l p• •s
q•

❀ Get Moving!

See if you can catch falling letters!
Write some letters on a small piece of paper and have your child stand in the middle of the room. Throw the letters above your child's head. See how many letters he or she can catch before they touch the ground. Can your child identify each letter?

Each uppercase letter has a
lowercase letter partner.
Lily and Tad are matching letter
partner socks.

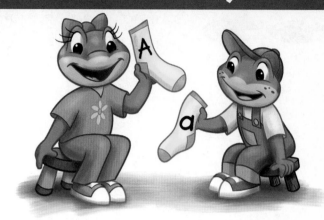

 Draw a line to match each uppercase letter with its
lowercase **letter partner**. Then, color the **letter
partner** socks to match.

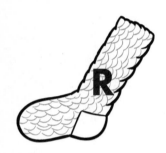   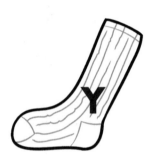 

R　　C　　V　　Y　　K

  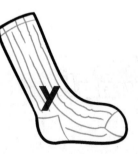  

v　　r　　y　　k　　c

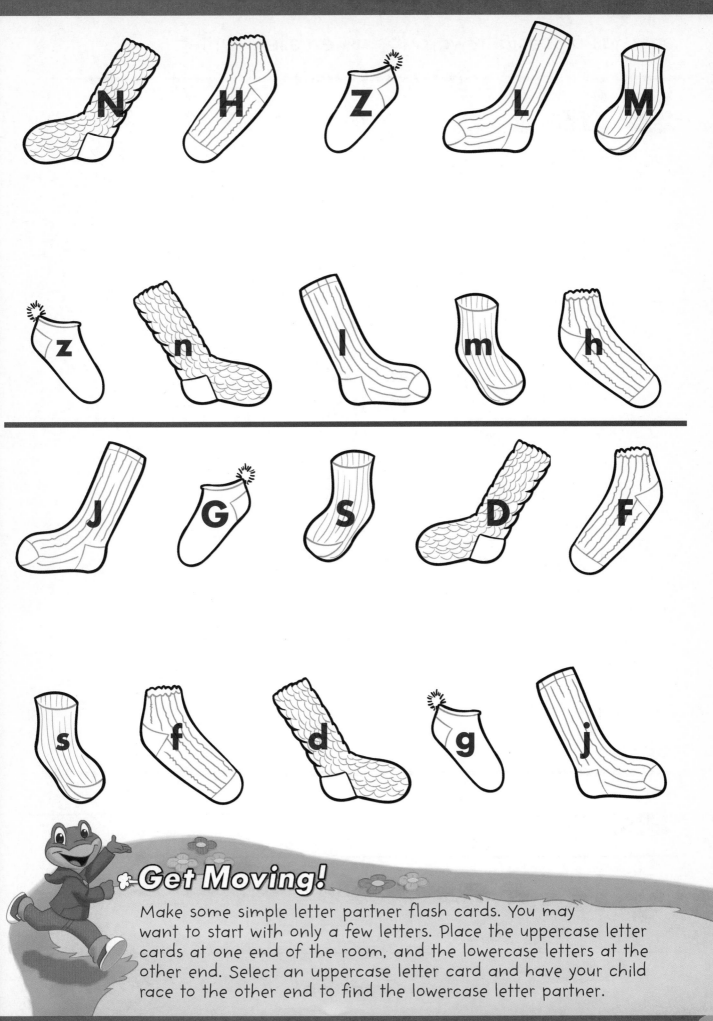

Get Moving!

Make some simple letter partner flash cards. You may want to start with only a few letters. Place the uppercase letter cards at one end of the room, and the lowercase letters at the other end. Select an uppercase letter card and have your child race to the other end to find the lowercase letter partner.

Leap has a special reward for an excellent writer.

 Trace the lines to complete the picture. Then, color it in.

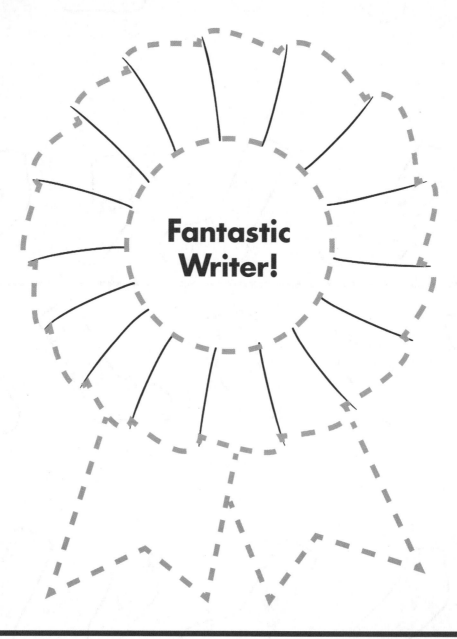

Fantastic Writer!

 Write your name on the line.

Great job!

Pre K Basic Skills

- Letters

- Numbers

- Same and Different

- Shapes

- Knowing Books

Pre K Basic Skills Parent Tips

Laundry Learning

Have fun learning *about* **same** and **different** while you sort the laundry with your child. Help your child match socks that are the **same** color, or find shirts that are **different** sizes. Use words like *big, bigger, small, smaller,* and *medium-sized* to compare different sizes. Have your child organize his or her clothes *by* putting all items of the **same** category in one pile or drawer. For example, you might encourage your child to place all of the long pants in one drawer and all of the sweatshirts in the closet. Try other sorting categories, like sorting clothes *by* color, season, or where they are worn on the body.

Get Moving! L-Left and R-Right

Play a game to help teach your child *about* **left** and **right**. Stand *behind* your child and hold your hands up in front of you, palm side down. Show your child that when you hold your hands this way with your thumbs out, the **left** hand makes the uppercase letter **L** (and emphasize that the **l** sound is at the *beginning* of the word **left**). Then explain to your child that you are going to say a word and if it *begins* with the **l** sound, he or she must wave the **left** hand and hop on the **left** foot. You may want to start with the following **l** sound words: *lime, lick, love, leaf, lemon, lost, life, lane.*

Shape Hunt

Go on a shape hunt with your child. Look through a magazine or newspaper and have your child trace the shapes he or she finds. For example, you may want to look for **circles** in pictures of car wheels, or **squares** and **rectangles** in tall office buildings. Try hunting for sizes and colors, too. Ask your child to find the **biggest** animal in the picture, or have your child circle all the things that are **blue**. Be creative with other categories, too.

Get Moving! In Out Up Down

Explain to your child that this activity involves moving to show opposites, or two actions that are completely different. Describe an opposite pair to get your child thinking (like **in-out, up-down, left-right, top-bottom, slow-fast**). You might say something like, "I can raise my hands **up** high. What can you do with your hands to show the opposite?" If your child needs help, prompt your child *by* showing how you can put your hands **down** near the ground. Then, repeat the opposite word pair for your child. You might say, "Right - **up** and **down** are opposites."

Take a Look at a Book

Reading with your child is one of the *best* ways to improve literacy and *build* vocabulary. When you *begin,* introduce your child to the author and illustrator for the *book,* and explain the role of each person. Encourage your child to tell the story *by* looking at the pictures, and ask questions like, "What do you think will happen next?" or "Where do you think the boy is going?" or "Why do you think she did that?" Review the story and see if your child can retell the story when you are finished reading.

Leap, Lily and Tad are on their way to the zoo. Help them find animals that are the **same**.

 Circle the pictures that are the **same** in each row.

Lily sees two animals that are the **same**.

 Draw a line to match the two animals that are the **same**.

• Recognizing things that are the same

These two animals are the **same** color.

Find two pictures that are the **same** in each row. Color them the **same color**.

Those birds look really **different**.

Circle the animal in each row that looks **different**.

• Recognizing things that are different

There are many **different** kinds of animals!

Circle the animal that looks **different** in each row.

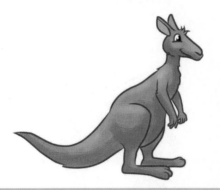

Leap notices that animals move in **different** ways.

In each row, color the animal that moves in a **different** way from the others.

*Get Moving!

Hop like a kangaroo and slither like a snake. Try moving like other animals. Pretend to fly, swim, prance, gallop or waddle. How many different ways can you move?

There are many shapes at the zoo.

 Trace each **circle** and **square**.

square

circle

ZOO

 Now, draw your own **circles** and **squares**.

It's snack time!

Leap's ice cream cone is in the shape of a **triangle**.

Grandpa's popsicle is in the shape of a **rectangle**.

 Trace each **triangle** and **rectangle**.

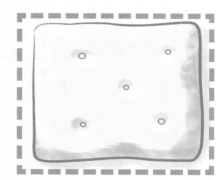  

 Now, draw your own **triangles** and **rectangles**.

Can you name the shapes?

 Use **blue** to color the shapes that are the same in each row.
Use **red** to color the shape that is different.

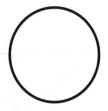  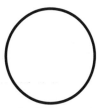 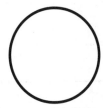

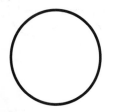 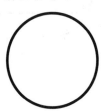 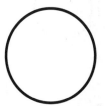

Lily and Tad want to ride the train!

 Use the color code to color the shapes on the train.

Get Moving!

Make a square on the floor with tape. Jump from side to side or from corner to corner. Try balancing on the lines as you walk around. Try it with other shapes, too. Make up your own game with the shapes!

• Identifying shapes • Visual discrimination • Physical activity • Creativity

An elephant is a **big** animal
and a squirrel is a **little** animal.

Color the **big** animals.
Circle the **little** animals.

Draw a picture of another **big** animal that you know.
Next to it, draw a **little** animal that you like.

Mom is **tall** and Tad is **short**.

short   **tall**

 Circle the **tall** animals.
Draw an X on the **short** animals.

 Circle the **tallest** member of the family.
Place an X on the **shortest** member of the family.

Leap's balloon string is **long**.   Lily's balloon string is **short**.

 Color the **long** animals **blue**. Color the **short** animals **green**.

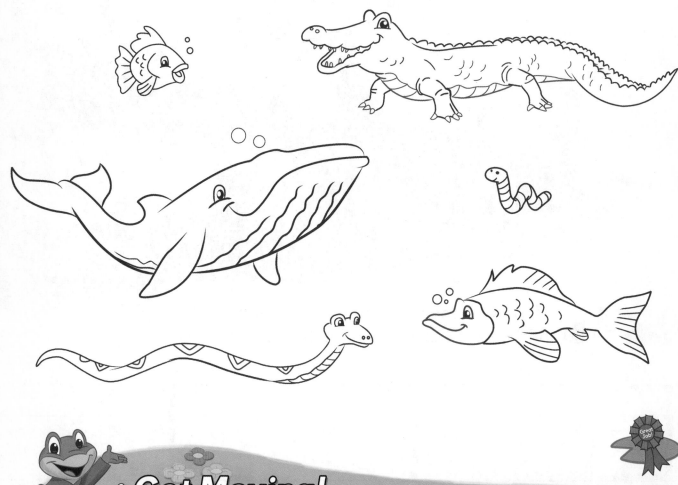

Get Moving!

Do the long jump! Put a five-foot strip of tape on the floor.
Start at one end of the tape and see how far you can jump.
Mark a line on the tape to show where you landed.
Try again and see if you can jump a longer distance.

Some letters have straight lines: E, F, H, I, L, T.

 Find and circle the letters with straight lines hidden in the picture (E, F, H, I, L, T).

 Practice tracing and writing some of the letters with straight lines (E, F, H, I, L, T).

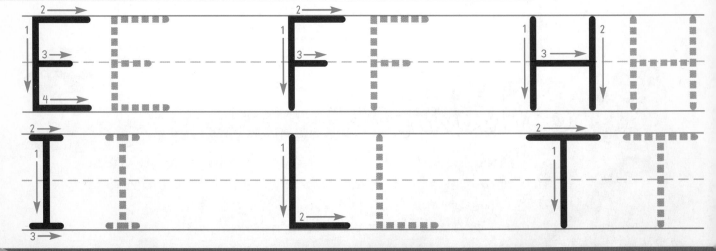

Some letters are rounded or curved: B, C, G, O, P, Q, S, U.

 Find and circle the rounded letters hidden in the picture (B, C, G, O, P, Q, S, U).

 Practice tracing and writing some of the rounded letters (B, C, G, O, P, Q, S, U).

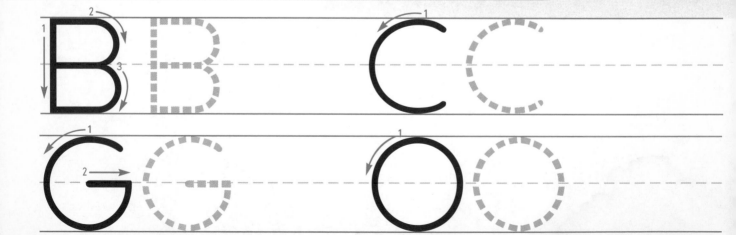

B B C C

G O

• Identifying letters • Visual discrimination • Tracing and writing letters

P P P

Q Q

S S S

U U

Letters have partners just like animals!

 Draw a line to match the letter partners.

A   M   N   V   W   K

k   w   a   m   v   n

Trace and write the letter partners.

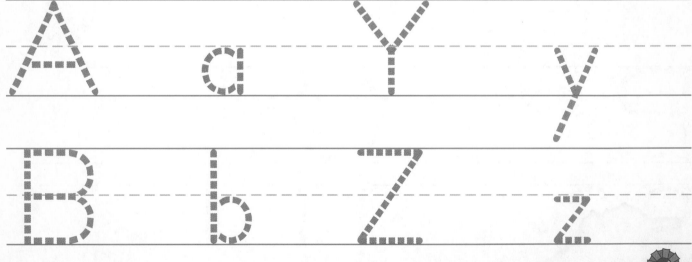

What is hiding?

Draw a line to connect the letters. Make sure you follow the letters in the correct order!

Help the bear find his cave.

Draw a line to follow the alphabet so the bear can get to his cave.

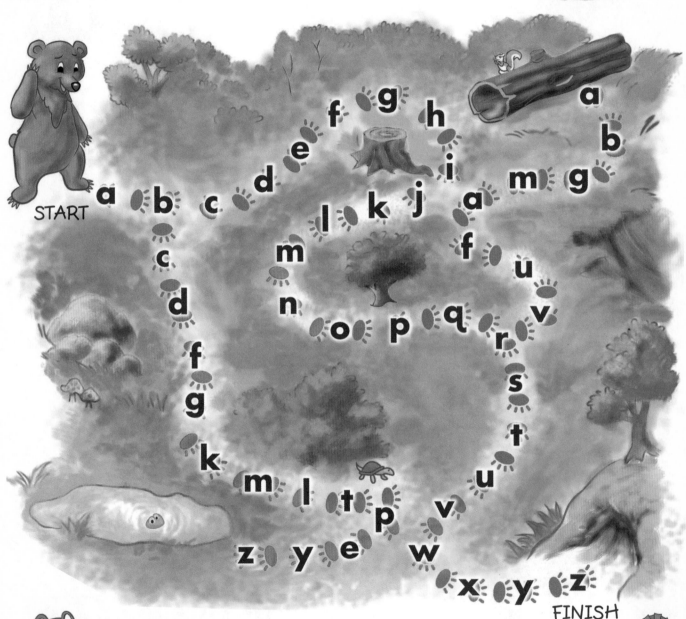

START

FINISH

Get Moving!

Try shaping your body like some of the letters of the alphabet. Can you make an A? L? O? I? S? Do the YMCA letter dance and then make up your own dance!

• Letter identification • Sequence of letters • Fine motor • Physical activity • Creativity

How many animals can you count?

 Count and draw a line to match the sets that have the same number of animals.

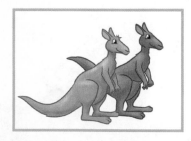

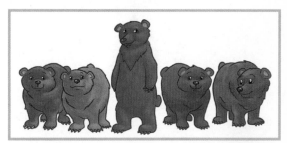

Parrots are so colorful!

Color the parrot using the color code.

1
2
3
4
5

Help count the animals.

Count and color the correct number of animals.

6

7

8

9

10

What animal likes to hop?

Draw a line to connect the numbers 1 to 10 to find out.

Color the picture.

5.

7.

6.
8.

4.

9.

3.

10.

2.

1.

Get Moving!

Hop like a kangaroo and count to 10. How many hops can you do before you get tired out? Try some big hops and little hops, long and short hops. What other animals hop?

One monkey is at the **top** of the tree and one is at the **bottom** of the tree.

top

bottom

Point to the **top** of this page.
Point to the **bottom** of this page.

  Trace and draw lines from **top** to **bottom**.

This is Leap's **left** hand.   This is Leap's **right** hand.

-- Trace and draw lines from **left** to **right**.

Get Moving!

Sing and dance the Hokey Pokey. Remember your left and right!
Make up your own song about left and right!

• Identifying left and right • Fine motor skills • Physical activity • Creativity

Tad is **first** in line and Lily is **last** in line to see the monkeys.

 Color the **first** one in each row **red** and the **last** one **blue**.

 Circle the **first** letter.
Draw an X on the **last** letter.

A   T   R   E   G   C

D   K   I

b   p   s   j

The **title**, or the name of Lily's favorite book is <u>A Zoo</u>. A **title** is usually on the front cover.

 Circle the **title** of each book.

An **author** is a person who writes a story. The **artist** or **illustrator** is a person who draws the pictures.

Color the **title** of this story.
Draw a line under the **author** of the book.
Draw a circle around the **illustrator**.

A Frog

Written by Tom Toad
Illustrated by Sue Snake

A story has a **beginning, middle,** and **end.**
The beginning happens **first,** the middle
happens **next,** and the end happens **last.**

Help put the stories in the correct order.
Write a 1, 2 and 3 to show which would
happen **first, next** and **last** in each row.

2   1   3

Practice telling what happens at the **beginning**, **middle**, and **end**.

 Write a 1, 2 and 3 to show which would happen **first**, **next** and **last** in each row.

_____   _____   _____

- - - - - - - - - - - - -   - - - - - - - - - - - - -   - - - - - - - - - - - - -

_____   _____   _____

_____   _____   _____

- - - - - - - - - - - - -   - - - - - - - - - - - - -   - - - - - - - - - - - - -

_____   _____   _____

_____   _____   _____

- - - - - - - - - - - - -   - - - - - - - - - - - - -   - - - - - - - - - - - - -

_____   _____   _____

Now it's your turn to be the **author** and **illustrator**!

Write a **title** for your story.
Draw a picture about your story in the **middle** of the book.
Color your illustration.
Write your name as the **author** and **illustrator**.

title

author

illustrator

• Review parts of a book • Following directions • Creativity

• Index •